APR 0 8 20

 W9-BFO-070

A Note to Parents

Dorling Kindersley Readers is a compelling new program for beginning readers, designed in conjunction with leading literacy experts, including Dr. Linda Gambrell, President of the National Reading Conference and past board member of the International Reading Association.

Beautiful illustrations and superb full-color photographs combine with engaging, easy-to-read stories to offer a fresh approach to each subject in the series. Each *Dorling Kindersley Reader* is guaranteed to capture a child's interest while developing his or her reading skills, general knowledge, and love of reading.

The four levels of *Dorling Kindersley Readers* are aimed at different reading abilities, enabling you to choose the books that are exactly right for your child:

Level 1 – Beginning to read
Level 2 – Beginning to read alone
Level 3 – Reading alone
Level 4 – Proficient readers

The "normal" age at which a child begins to read can be anywhere from three to eight years old, so these levels are intended only as a general guideline.

No matter which level you select, you can be sure that you are helping your child learn to read, then read to learn!

Dorling Kindersley

LONDON, NEW YORK, SYDNEY, DELHI, PARIS,
MUNICH, and JOHANNESBURG

A DORLING KINDERSLEY BOOK
www.dk.com

Produced by Southern Lights
Custom Publishing

For Dorling Kindersley
Publisher Andrew Berkhut
Executive Editor Andrea Curley
Art Director Tina Vaughan
Photographer Howard L. Puckett

Reading Consultant
Linda Gambrell, Ph.D.

First American Edition, 2001
00 01 02 03 04 05 10 9 8 7 6 5 4 3 2 1
Published in the United States by
Dorling Kindersley Publishing, Inc.
95 Madison Avenue, New York, New York 10016

Published in Great Britain by Dorling Kindersley Limited.

Library of Congress Cataloging-in-Publication Data

Hayward, Linda
    A day in the life of a dancer / by Linda Hayward. -
1st American ed.
    p. cm. -- (Dorling Kindersley readers)
    Audience:"Level 1, preschool-grade 1."
    ISBN 0-7894-7370-4—ISBN 0-7894-7369-0 (pbk.)
    1. Ballet--Juvenile literature. 2.Dance Schools-Juvenile
literature.[1. Ballet dancing.] I. Title. II. Series.

GV1787.5 .H39 2001
792.8--dc21   00-055523

Printed and bound in China by L. Rex Printing Co., Ltd.

The characters and events in this story are fictional and do not
represent real persons or events. The author would like to
thank E. J. Lopresti for her help. Special thanks to Libba Owen
and the Alabama Ballet.

see our complete
catalog at
www.dk.com

DORLING KINDERSLEY *READERS*

A Day in the Life of a Dancer

Written by Linda Hayward

A Dorling Kindersley Book

9:00 a.m.

Lisa Torres
fills her bag.

leotard

Leg warmers.
Leotard.
Tights.
Four pairs
of shoes.

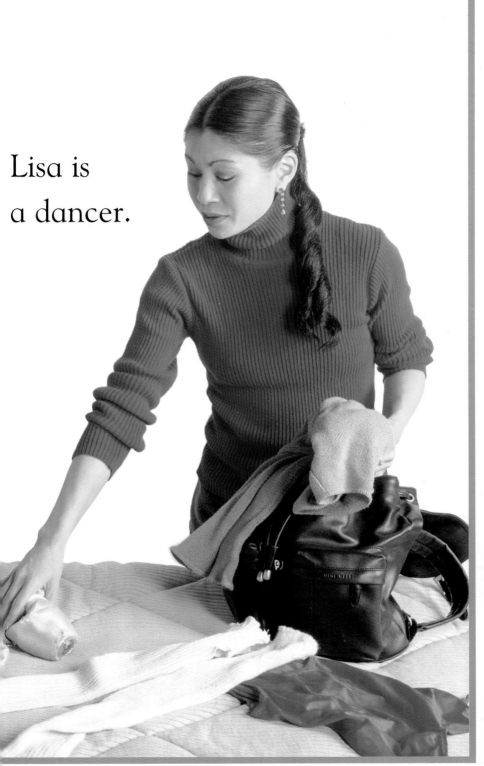

Lisa is
a dancer.

Lisa walks to the ballet company.

9:30 a.m.

In the locker room, she puts on her toe shoes.

toe shoes

Before class,
Lisa warms up
at the barre.

barre

10:00 a.m.

The teacher comes
into the studio.
The class is practicing
ballet steps.
They practice
over and over.

The teacher watches
as the dancers move.

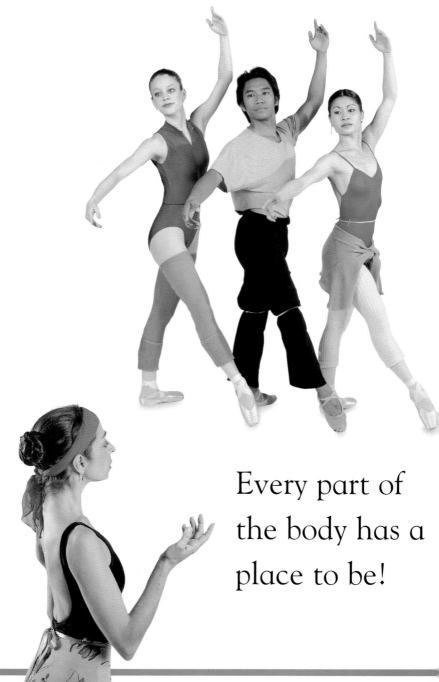

Every part of
the body has a
place to be!

Lisa spins on the tip of her toe. The teacher says, "Keep your shoulders low!"

Lisa practices a pirouette again and again.

pirouette

Each step, each movement goes with the music.

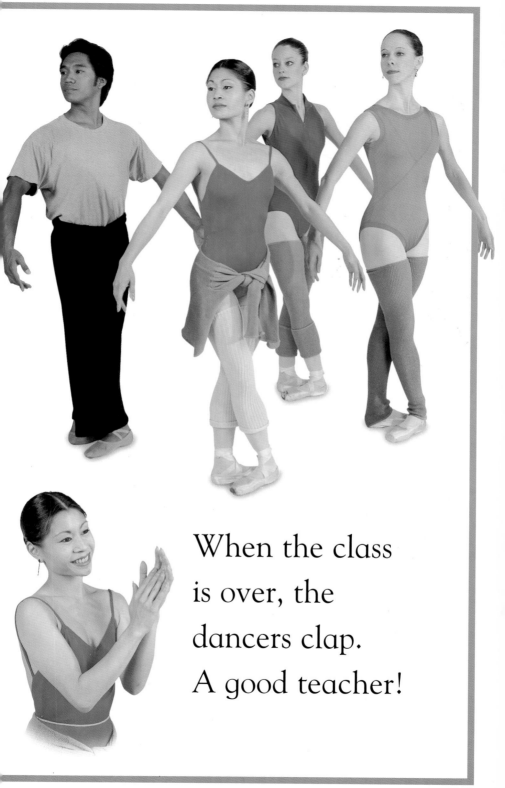

When the class
is over, the
dancers clap.
A good teacher!

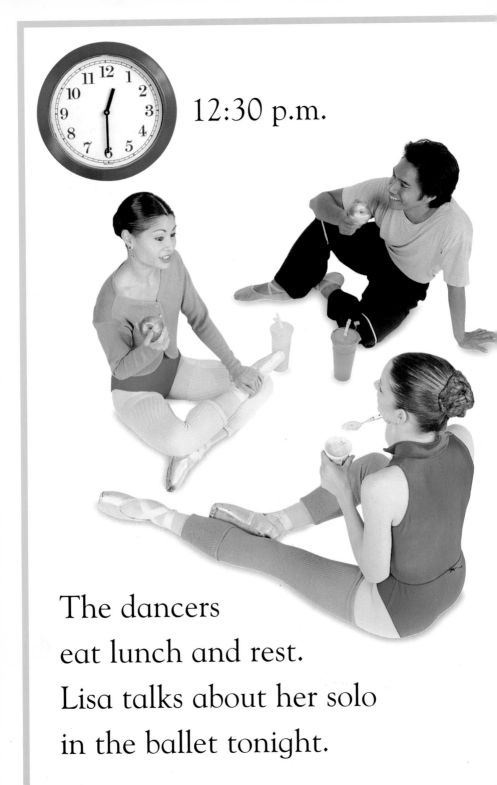

12:30 p.m.

The dancers
eat lunch and rest.
Lisa talks about her solo
in the ballet tonight.

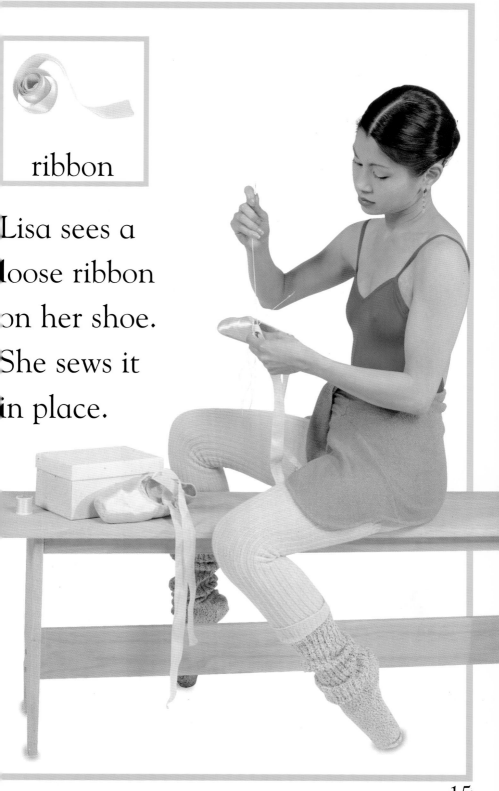

ribbon

Lisa sees a loose ribbon on her shoe. She sews it in place.

15

1:00 p.m.

Lisa puts on her tutu and goes to the studio for rehearsal.

tutu

The dance master watches as Lisa rehearses her solo. Feel the music!

Lisa has been practicing for months. She wants to do her best.

5:00 p.m.

Lisa has a snack in the studio and thinks about being on stage. She will wear her favorite pearl earrings for good luck.

Lisa walks to the theater.
There is her roommate.
Lisa forgot her lucky pearl
earrings!

What a good friend!

Lisa puts on her makeup and her pearl earrings.

costume

Then she puts on her costume.

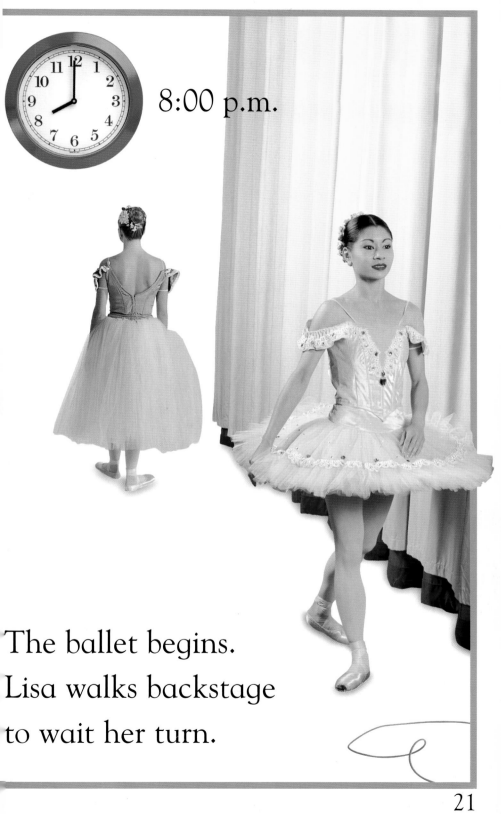

8:00 p.m.

The ballet begins.
Lisa walks backstage
to wait her turn.

21

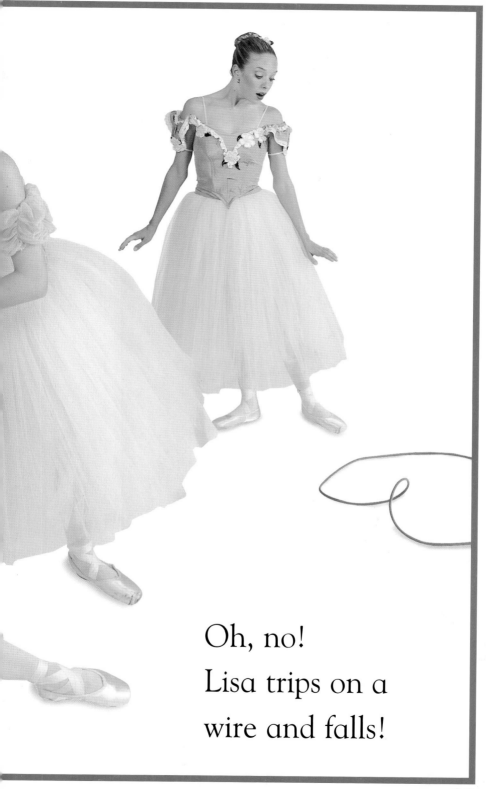

Oh, no!
Lisa trips on a
wire and falls!

Is Lisa hurt?

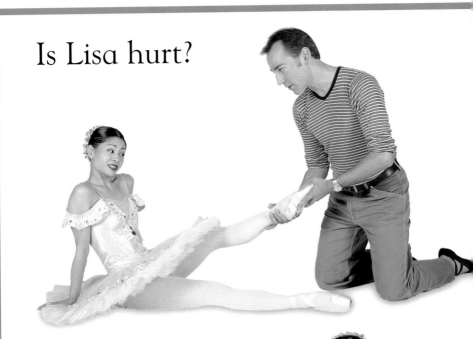

It is almost time
for her to dance!

Lisa stands.
She is not hurt!
She is ready
just in time.

She feels
the music
as she
walks onto
the stage.

Lisa dances
her best tonight.
She feels light
from her toes
to the tips
of her fingers!

The ballet ends.
Bravo! Bravo!
Lisa gives a
beautiful bow.

bow

10:00 p.m.

Backstage, the dance
master gives Lisa a rose.
A great performance!

Lisa and her roommate walk home together.

11:00 p.m.

It's bedtime but they can't stop talking. Lisa was so brave! The ballet was so beautiful!

Lisa thinks about her moment on stage. She smiles. She has the best job in the world!

Picture Word List

leotard

page 4

ribbon

page 15

toe shoes

page 7

tutu

page 16

barre

page 8

costume

page 20

pirouette

page 11

bow

page 28